CHELTENHAM
PEOPLE AND PLACES 1960s TO 1980s

The Willow Wonder
England cricketer, Tom Graveney and his wife Jackie, behind the bar of the Royal Oak Prestbury in 1974. They became landlords of the popular village inn on returning from Australia, where Tom and his family had emigrated in 1970 after being offered the post of player/coach in Queensland.

CHELTENHAM
PEOPLE AND PLACES 1960s TO 1980s

THE PHOTOGRAPHS OF MICHAEL CHARITY

Knight of the Road

We knew summer had arrived, when Fred Abel's one-man circus pitched up in town. Each year he would travel from the West Country, giving impromptu roadside performances from his horse-drawn cart. Children, in return for a few pence, would look on in amazement as a pair of rats ran out of a teapot, across his shoulders, then back again! For an encore his dog, Bow-Wow, would balance for ages on his back legs, and that would be it - the show was over. You could never get away from this genial gentleman without being shown his collection of fading, rat nibbled, press cuttings acquired over years of life on the road. Summers without Fred are not quite the same.

First published 2001
Copyright © Michael Charity, 2001

Tempus Publishing Limited
The Mill, Brimscombe Port,
Stroud, Gloucestershire, GL5 2QG

ISBN 0 7524 2232 4

Typesetting and origination by
Tempus Publishing Limited
Printed in Great Britain by
Midway Clark Printing, Wiltshire

This book is for Derek Evans, a photographer whose experience, skill and enthusiasm rubbed off on those who were fortunate enough to learn the cameraman's craft at his Herefordshire agency. His dedicated training style produced some excellent photographers, many of whom have since achieved success in the realms of photo-journalism. I will always be indebted to him for giving me the opportunity to enter this often privileged and ever fascinating world of news gathering.

Introduction

It's almost unbelievable that forty years have passed since I first came to Cheltenham equipped with a Japanese copy of the classic German Rollieflex, a rattling old Ford Popular car and the abounding optimism of the young. Despite being told by the first person I met, ironically also a photographer, that I would never make a living and certainly would not last long - I am still here and still taking pictures! Despite this somewhat shaky start, the forty mile move from the Hereford news agency of Derek Evans, the man who gave me the opportunity and training to break away from a mundane job, was an extremely successful one. I soon made some acquaintances and eventually many friends, from various walks of life, friends whose information and help were instrumental in establishing my name in Fleet Street and the world of news gathering. The warm welcomes I received during those initial months certainly didn't correspond to the advice I had received from my home town comrades that, 'Cheltenham was a snobby place'.

During the four decades since, there have naturally been many changes. Cheltenham has successfully rediscovered itself, shrugging off the crumbling 'Poor, Proud and Pretty' image of the 1950s, to become a thriving multi-million pound commercial and tourist centre, worthy of the title 'Centre for the Cotswolds'.

Michael Charity. (photograph: Richard Sturdy)

Four Chief Constables have come and gone, I have rubbed shoulders with three generations of police officers pounding the beat, witnessed criminals go down and watched the famous rise. My relentless camera shutter has fired a million times or more, recording images and events that have shaped people's lives and remodelled the town and its outlying areas. Because of its very nature, photo-journalism does not make for a very ordered lifestyle, chaos is the norm! I have been very fortunate that my partner Gillian, herself a trained photographer, understands the addiction, the opium-like effect of news gathering, Without the understanding and comprehension of a soul mate who understood that this was not a nine to five job, it would have been impossible to consider such a bizarre career, coupled with marriage. She kindly offered, in spite of a twenty-year gap from the 'black hole', to re-enter our hastily reassembled darkroom to produce the monochrome prints required for this book.

I would like to think that this collection of photographs, as well as being a nostalgic mirror to the way we were, can also be a way of saying 'Thank You' to the many people and organisations who have helped me since 1962. They are far too numerous to mention individually but I am sure they will all know who they are.

Irish Eyes are Smiling
The Irish part of the crowd was ecstatic when *Dawn Run*, ridden by Jonjo O'Neill, won the Cheltenham Gold Cup in 1986.

The Racehorse Trainer (above)
Owen O'Neill, seen with one of his charges,
Impeccable Timing, at the Cleeve Lodge
stables he took over in 1969.

Taking it Seriously (top right)
Princess Anne, patron of Cotswold Riding
for the Disabled, meets some of the
organization's young riders in the late 1970s
at their headquarters in Prestbury Park,
Cheltenham.

Speeding Wheelchairs (right)
Princess Anne prepares to take part in
wheelchair races organised in 1984 at
Cheltenham Racecourse to raise monies for
the Injured Jockeys Fund.

Following Form
A coy Princess Diana led by Sir Desmond Plummer, Chairman of the Levy Board, makes her way with Prince Charles through the crowds, during the 1981 Gold Cup meeting. Behind the Princess is Sir Piers Bengough, a director of the Cheltenham Racecourse Company.

Here's Mud In Your Eye (right)
The weather was not kind to Princess Anne on her first ride during an evening meeting at Prestbury Park. At the onset of the race in 1983, the heavens opened causing the Princess, who was trailing the field, to get the full force of the hoof-thrown mud. My picture next day made the front page of *The Times* but the real glory should go to *Echo* photographer, the late Richard Sturdy. His experience of all things racing told him that the best pictures would be obtained at the end of the race, We scrambled through the storm and by sheer luck of positioning, I got the best shot.

The Cup That Cheers (far right)
Her Majesty The Queen Mother looks on with glee, as Gold Cup winning jockey, Jonjo O'Neill, raises the Gold Cup in a victory salute after his success on *Dawn Run* at the 1986 meeting.

The Winner!
Jonjo O'Neill on *Dawn Run* is led into the unsaddling enclosure at Prestbury Park in 1986. The Irish always hope for a home country winner at Cheltenham and this day their dreams came true. Spectators are not supposed to enter the unsaddling area but on this day they did!

Flying Visit
Colonel Martin Gibb, Lord Lieutenant of Gloucestershire (right), accompanies Prince Charles and Lady Diana as they arrive by helicopter on the sports field at Dean Close School for a visit in 1981.

Youthful Cheek
The day of the visit to Dean Close was also the day that the Queen announced that Prince Charles and Diana were to be married. As the Princess-to-be walked past a line of sixth-formers, one cocky lad lent forward and requested that he kiss the hand of his future queen! The gesture made headlines the next day! Little did anyone know at the time the Princess would never be Queen.

A Stitch In Time
Young Peter Phillips, son of Princess Anne and Captain Mark Phillips, was spotted standing alone amid a crowd of race-goers at Cheltenham racecourse in the early 1980s, (a little attention may have been required to the hem of his raincoat when he got home!)

Musical Voices
A pre-show publicity photograph taken for the Cotswold Savoyards' production of Gilbert and Sullivan's *The Mikado* in 1965. Members of the cast, who are wearing some very 1960s-looking gear, are (left to right), David Churchill, Ann Cox, Anthony Jones, Barbara Fennell, Pat Manifold and Eric Coles. The society was formed in 1962 and has been blessed, over the years, with many talented singers enabling their productions to achieve high musical standards.

Fashion Princess
Princess Margaret presents raffle prizes during a fashion show held at the Cheltenham Ladies College, in aid of the NSPCC, in 1982. The event was organized and presented by the town's Tizzie Dee fashion house and was compèred by Paul Tizzard, seen here announcing the winners.

Bonnets Galore
Madame Beatrice Taylor founded a millinery store at 48- 50 The Strand, on the upper High Street,in 1910. These timeless premises, were always filled with splendid displays of hats for all occasions, evoking images of a gentler era. This is Mrs Cherry Hawkins, the founder's daughter, who ran the shop until it closed down on her retirement in 1988, amidst a selection of hats in 1979.

The Hardboard Artist
Cheltenham artist Ian Hunter and his wife Sally, who featured in much of his work, pictured in l967 at their home and studio. He was a brilliant painter who created striking portraits, often set against powerful industrial landscapes. His preferred medium was oils on hardboard instead of canvas, thus saving on material costs! I photographed many of the paintings for him and he occasionally paid me with art. To this day, his paintings still hang in our home.

The Clock Maker
Time has never stood still for clockmaker Mike Harding. Mike (left) with assistant Mel Evans is seen making last minute adjustments to one of his beautiful skeleton clocks at their workshop in Lansdown Place Lane in 1976. A craft member of the British Horologist Institute and Freeman of the Worshipful Company of Clockmakers of London, Mike's clocks, long case, bracket and skeleton, were much sort after, world wide.

Tailor Made Art
Jesse Heyden was a debonair man, which was only to be expected, being a Saville Row trained tailor who turned out fine garments for Cheltenham clients. But his real love was painting and at his bespoke premises, Heydens of Cheltenham, he had a studio. He is seen here in 1965, amid some examples of his prolific output. I first befriended him at the Cheltenham Theatre and Arts Club, where most evenings he could be found enjoying good conversation and a glass of beer. I often produced photographs of his subjects from which he worked between sittings. He once gave me a gilt-framed painting of Lady Hamilton and the Victorian table at which I am currently writing!

Brush Strokes (right)
Cheltenham artist Hilary Baker, in 1982, with two very striking portraits of Sir John Hackett, the military historian.

The Wood Sculptor (far right)
Sculptor Ian Norbury, was photographed here in 1980 at the White Knight Gallery in Painswick Road. He hand carved his way to acclaim with his delicate, sculptures, often based on a Medieval theme. One of Britain's premier exponents of the art, his carvings commanded sums in excess of £2,000 from collectors. He was invited to Switzerland, a traditional home of woodcarving, to give a series of lectures to students on the craft!

Mouth Watering Music
Cheltenham harmonica player, Brian Chaplin appeared with harmonica virtuoso Larry Adler in a concert at The Lions Club Charity Ball at the Pump Rooms in 1972. Brian, who studied for eight years with that other great British virtuoso Tommy Reilly, won the British Harmonica Championships in 1968 and went on to win the title again on two further occasions.

A Literary Politician (far left)
Labour leader Michael Foot was one of the gentlest politicians I have ever met. Here he is taking a cup of tea at the Cheltenham Festival in 1988.

Book Mad (left)
Cheltenham antiquarian bookseller, Alan Hancox was one of the founding fathers of the town's now famous literary festival. He joined the committee in 1959 and was artistic director on several occasions throughout the 1980s. Alan is pictured here introducing a guest speaker. He enjoyed the company of writers and loved to be pictured with them, something that made my job, when covering the festival, so much easier!

A Historic Meeting
Alan Hancox chats with historian E.P. Thompson in 1989.

Flying High
Peter Powell demonstrates one of his revolutionary Stunter kites in the early 1970s, shortly before the design was put on the market. Soon world wide-orders were flooding into his tiny Leckhampton workshops. If there was no wind during one of his popular demonstrations, for which he became famous, Peter created some by launching the kites from an open-topped Citroen 2CV!

Taxing Move
Top golfer Tony Jacklin and his wife Viv caught in the midst of moving from their home near Cleeve Hill in l975, when they decamped from Gloucestershire to Jersey in order to beat the tax man!

The Antique Man (above)
Arthur Negus. worked for antique dealers Bruton Knowles when in the 1960s he was invited to take part in a pilot production for a BBC Bristol programme. His knowledge and West Country charm revealed him to be a television natural. and the pilot turned into the long running, *Going For A Song.*

Sally and Worzel (above right)
Actress Una Stubbs at the Cotswold Farm Park in 1982. This pair of rare Gloucester cattle twins, were named Aunt Sally and Worzel Gummage, after the characters played by Jon Pertwee and Una Stubbs in the TV show.

Heavenly Body (right)
The Archbishop of Canterbury's envoy, Terry Waite, collects a newly rebuilt MG sports car, from a Cheltenham firm of restorers in the early 1980s. Shortly afterwards, while on a trip to the Lebanon, he was kidnapped and imprisoned for five years.

Dressed to Kill
Gordon Wilkins, motoring journalist and presenter of the popular BBC *Wheelbase* programme during the 1960s and '70s, with his wife Joyce. He appeared at all the exotic locations chosen for the launch of new models and attended the sparkling functions arranged by the luminaries of the world's motoring marques. He delights in telling of an incident that occurred to her on the way to a reception in Rome. His wife, who was apparently wearing a splendid but somewhat revealing gown, broke down en route. Climbing out of the motor, she stood in the middle of one of Rome's busy streets to flag down a cab - the sight of this tall raven-haired girl in distress, and in that dress, caused four Latin drivers to crash their cars, bringing the whole highway to a standstill. She then climbed calmly into a cab and disappeared into the twilight!

House of Dolls (right)
Sally Turner with some of her collection of Victorian and Edwardian dolls, in 1977. Sally, twenty-one years old here, worked in her parents antique shop in Montpellier and had many of these valuable toys, including two that once belonged to the girl on whom Lewis Carroll based *The Adventures of Alice in Wonderland*.

Stage Struck (above)
Rae Hammond, former colonial officer and member of the Magic Circle, became General Manager of the Everyman Theatre. Here he is in the 1970s, struggling to fit a pantomime costume into the boot of his car, one trick that he was unable to achieve!

Sharpshooter (right)
George Gilbert opened his Winchcome Street camera shop in 1954, after being a photographer with the 8th Army during the war. The walls and cabinets of his shop were filled with photographic memorabilia, making it a Mecca for camera enthusiasts. His vast experience was another good reason for photographers to knock on his door. Cheltenham Cameras closed on his retirement in the early 1990s.

Artist in Plaster (left)
Bill Maxwell was one of Cheltenham's characters and lived in a tiny apartment in Montpellier Terrace. A plasterer by trade, his building skills ranged from the brilliant to the chaotic, depending on whether he was drinking tea or something stronger! For all his faults he was a lovable rascal and many of us who lived in the terrace during the 1960s were grateful for his skills in keeping the crumbling fabric of our homes glued together.

The Exciting Councillor (far left)
Dudley Aldridge was something of an outspoken and controversial figure in Cheltenham politics. He often livened up dull council meetings during his thirty-four years as councillor becoming mayor of the town in 1976 and standing as Liberal candidate for the town in 1970. During his campaign he managed to get his 'Vote For Aldridge' daubed Jaguar past barricades to be the first vehicle to use a new bypass, to the astonishment of the official opening party! He is pictured here in 1979 making a welcoming speech for a party of Russians visiting Cheltenham from the twinned town of Sochi.

A Lordly Wedding
Kathryn Mary Eccles gets a helping hand with her veil from her husband, Lord Vestey, after their marriage at Northleach church in 1970. A member of one of the richest families in the country, Lord Vestey set up home with his wife at Stowell Park, near Cheltenham.

Tarzan In Lights
Tory cabinet minister Michael Heseltine, visited the new Countryside Commission Headquarters in Cheltenham's former police station in 1980. I captured him on film as he paused below this 'halo' of lights on his way out to return to London. The picture subsequently appeared in *The Observer.* Some years later, during a private visit to the home of Sir Charles Irving, I met him and presented him with a copy of the photograph but I got the impression that he was not amused by it!

A Son of Cheltenham
Councillor, alderman and three times mayor of Cheltenham, the town's favourite, Charles Irving, became Member of Parliament in 1974. He's pictured here on the steps of the town hall, where he received some direct hits with eggs! He was MP for the town for seventeen years, served forty eight years on the Borough Council and was knighted during Margaret Thatcher's government. A former chef, his mother owned the Irving Hotel in Bath Road. He took charge of the House of Commons catering organisation, which at the time had debts of £3 million, and turned it into a £1 million a year profit. On his death in 1995 a helicopter was used to scatter his ashes over the town he loved and the Charles Irving Trust has since done much to help the disadvantaged of Gloucestershire.

Not Quite Lloyd George
Liberal Party Leader Jeremy Thorpe, saying goodbye to his supporters outside the Queens Hotel after his visit to the town in the 1967. He arrived wearing a homburg hat and flourishing a cigar - but refused to let me photograph him in a Churchillian pose! The hat and the cigar had disappeared when it was time for him to leave and I took this photograph.

Labouring the Point
Prime Minister, Harold Wilson seen
amid the Victorian splendour of
Cheltenham town hall, during a
lecture he gave in 1984 to a
conference of a local industrialists.

Tory Stronghold
Conservative candidate Sir Dodds-Parker, raises his arm in a victory salute after winning the Cheltenham seat in the 1970 election. The Mayor of Cheltenham, Aimbury Dodwell, is seen in the picture with Mr Crabtree the town clerk. Aimbury, a local builder and long time member of the Borough Council, regularly donned a red coat and white beard, each festive season, to become the town's Father Christmas.

Princess at School
Princess Alexandra chats with pupils during a visit to Dean Close school in 1986. Just behind her is the head, Christopher Bacon and the tall gentleman standing quietly in the background, is Bruce Stevens, a member of the Gloucestershire Police Force's Royal Protection Team, who became a good friend through the many royal visits that I covered.

Tory Ted (above)
Prime Minister Edward Heath, in expansive mood at the lectern during a speech he gave to the 'Management and Professional Associations in Gloucestershire' at the town hall in 1983. These big name events were organised by Gordon Pettit and Jeffery Baguley of Dowty's, with just a little help from Charles Irving MP, whose connections in The House were useful for arranging visits by luminaries from the world of politics.

The Concerned Prince (right)
The Duke of Edinburgh meets students from the National Star Centre during a Duke of Edinburgh Award Scheme display given at the Gloucestershire County Council Conference and Training Centre in 1979 at Cowley Manor.

The Young Prince (left)
A youthful Prince Charles, deep in conversation with a resident of Daglingworth village during a visit in 1969, just prior to his twenty first birthday.

Royal Walkabout
Prince Charles, accompanied by the Duke of Beaufort, strides through the village of Daglingworth, part of the Duchy of Cornwall estate, during his visit in 1969. On the left, one of his detectives restrains an over eager young girl who is considered to be getting too far ahead of the royal visitor!

Sunday Best
Former council worker and part-time chimney sweep, Jack Cook, waits patiently at the village hall in Daglingworth for the arrival of Prince Charles. He was due to meet the young prince over tea in the hall during his visit to the estate in 1969.

What a Swell Party
When Audrey Truscott's husband died in 1972 she turned to charity work. As a young girl she had experienced the world of London Society; her father was King's Messenger between the Court of St James and the Court of Romania. She moved with ease in high society and set about organising fund-raising parties, dinners and balls in fine hotels and great houses across the county. Her guest lists included lords, earls, duchesses, princes and princesses and Audrey raised a considerable amount of money for local and national charities. At this event are, from left to right, Gillian Rose of Sue Ryder Homes, Audrey Truscott, Don Perry, Mayor of Cheltenham, Lady Ryder of Warsaw, creator of Sue Ryder Homes, Sally Duchess of Westminster at whose Wickwar home the party was held, and Lucinda Green.

Taking The Waters
In 1982, Countess Spencer (left) chairman of the British Tourist Authority, was guest at the Savoy Hotel to sample the local spa waters. She is seen here with Basil Pantin (centre) also of the BTA, with Tony and Christine Walliman of the Savoy Hotel (holding the water jar and tray). Behind them is Cheltenham councillor Aimbury Dodwell and, behind the Countess, is Mike Rayward, the town's director of tourism.

The Soldier
General Sir John Hackett poses for my camera at his home near Cheltenham in the late 1970s. The general, an accomplished soldier and scholar with a glittering military career, commanded NATO forces and wrote a best selling book, *The Third World War*, which was published at the height of the cold war.

Lace Lady
Fashion designer Olivia Dell, modelling one of the Victorian-style dresses she began making during the early 1970s from her home in Andover Road. She travelled widely to obtain rare materials for her designs and in 1974 opened a gown shop, Cocoa, in Queens Circus,. She created one-off 'Victorian' bridal dresses, that sold in London, Amsterdam, New York and Florida to the glitterati. Among her clients were the King of Jordan's sister and pop star Lulu.

My Goodness - My Guinness
In August 1970 British engineer George Watts was released from a Chinese prison cell after three years for allegedly spying in China while working at a petrochemical plant. I followed the story and had visited his Hatherley home so it was natural that on his release I was there to witness his homecoming. When I suggested that my journalist colleague and I should treat the family to a Chinese meal he accepted immediately! For a man incarcerated for three years without drink I was amazed at his capacity to down sherry, wine and pints of Guinness! After the meal he suggested a pub and we moved onto rounds of whiskey at the Hatherley Inn after which George was still standing but we were the worst for wear! On the following day my colleague and I, still nursing bad heads, bumped into him at the offices of *The Daily Mirror.* Not only was he looking very fresh but he greeted us with, 'Hi boys, fancy a lunchtime drink!' In the picture is his wife Josephine, their daughter, Christine and son, Stephen.

Beetle Noises (right)
In the early 1960s cowman Ray Goodwin, who worked on a Cowley farm near Cheltenham, hit the headlines by winning a BBC radio sound competition with his recording of a dung beetle buried deep inside a cow-pat! His homemade parabolic microphone was created from an aluminium dustbin lid – there's ingenuity for you.

A Dogs Life (right and top right)
One of the most endearing characters in the streets of Montpellier during the 1960s was Fido the dog. Fido was owned by Len and Anne Hennessy of the Salisbury Arms but the independent pooch had his own ideas. Every morning he followed an itinerary: call at Laights, the butchers for a morsel of meat, pop into Chappells cake shop for a doughnut, visit Belchers tobacconists for a Mars Bar and then go for a nap amid the elegant furniture at Turner's Antiques. Evenings would find him visiting The Salisbury, just to keep in touch, before enjoying a pleasant night's company in the snug at Peters Bar. Fido is seen here in 1967, with Len and Anne Hennessy and John Turner, during one of his rare visits to his home at the Salisbury!

The Film Star
Actress Susan George posed for me in pensive mood in the car park at the Waddon Road football ground after she had helped kick-off a Celebrity Eleven charity soccer match in 1968.

Shadow Marriage
Cheltenham-born, former bass guitarist with the Shadows, Jet Harris, got married for the third time in 1975 in the registry office at the town's municipal buildings. The thirty-three year old musician is here with his twenty-five year old bride, nurse Margaret Johnston. There was a party afterwards in Doris's Cafe in Royal Crescent. The cafe, a well known and popular eatery at the time is now sadly only a memory.

Dancing Queen (right)
Janet Lister of the Lister Dance Studios in Cheltenham's Pittville district in 1965. These studios were a popular venue for those who wanted to be fleet of foot on the dance floor! Established in the 1950s by Janet's parents Frank and Janet Lister, the name continued when Janet later took over the business. The studio offered traditional ballroom dance lessons but Janet also choreographed and led a troupe of popular cabaret dancers.

Blond Bombshell
The Cheltenham electrical wholesalers, R.A. Poole brought more than a little bit of glamour to their business when they invited film star, Diana Dors, to open the company's new showrooms in the 1960s. Diana, in one of her classic poses (top), toasts the camera and (right) with staff and guests at the reception.

Beauty and the Beer
Miss World 1975, Wilnelia Merced from Peurto Rica, visited Whitbread's brewery in Cheltenham during her tour of Britain. Whitbread's Sales Promotion Manager, Mike Roff, was responsible for arranging this publicity coup for the brewery. She was treated to fish and chips in the staff dining room and drank a pint of bitter with the staff. I had no difficulty in encouraging a few of the lads to pose with the visitor!

Flower Girl
Sarah Fox, of Winchcombe, was a trainee gardener with Cheltenham Borough Council and the only girl on the staff of thirty men. Sarah is seen here in the Municipal Gardens in 1982 preparing Cheltenham for the annual Britain in Bloom Competition.

Spring Beauty

The Black Tulip Restaurant in the 1960s had an elegant first floor lounge with views across the Promenade and was a popular meeting place for morning coffee. I was a regular! One of the attractions of the place for me was a tall, young waitress called Shirley Morley, who with her good looks and long dark hair had always struck me as a portrait waiting to be taken. One morning in 1964, during a lull in trade, I plucked up courage and asked her to pose for me. This is one of the photographs that resulted from this impromptu session. Sometime later, this picture was included in an exhibition of my work at Geraldines, another coffee house in the Prom, which sadly, like the Black Tulip, has now been turned into a pub.

Black Magic

I remember reading somewhere in the mid-1960s that the Beatles most admired exponent of the guitar was a certain Jimi Hendrix, a musician relatively unknown in this country, and to me, at the time. A little later an advertisement in the 'What's On' columns in Cheltenham in 1965 announced that he was appearing at The Blue Moon Night Club, a small club above Burton's the Tailors in the High Street. Hendrix had suddenly become a big name but had been booked by the club in good time. Despite his growing fame he honoured the contract and turned up to play a storming performance in this tiny, crowded venue in a former billiards hall above the gent's outfitters. I was the only photographer!

Stones at the Odeon (far left) Charlie Watts and Bill Wyman of the Rolling Stones arrive at the Odeon cinema in Winchcombe Street for a concert in 1964. Locked gates protected the stars from the fans .

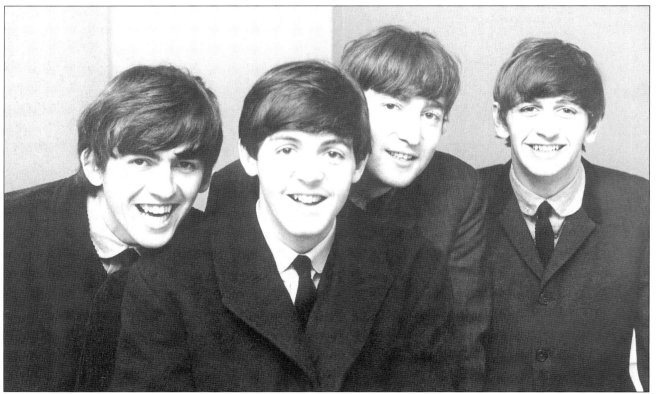

The Beatles
In November 1963 the Fab Four hit town with two performances at the Odeon Cinema that almost brought the house down. From the time they came on stage to the end of the show there was constant screaming from the hundreds of fans who packed the theatre. This picture was taken back stage at the cinema before the show.

Lulu in Town (opposite top and right)
Lulu at the Town Hall in 1965. There
was a surprising innocence around the
pop stars of the Sixties. They were
often quite approachable and
frequently lacked the minders and
publicity managers of today.
Professional photographers were much
thinner on the ground. When the
Beatles came to the Odeon there were
only three cameramen at the photo call!
It was no problem to wander into the
Town Hall, knock on the star's dressing
room and request pictures, something I
was never refused at the time. Thus
when Lulu, the bubbly Scottish singer
came to town, as with Jimmy
Hendrix's visit, I was the only
photographer. I had the place to myself,
able to record her visit both behind the
scenes and from the front of stage, a
luxury that would be impossible today.
Incidentally, notice the primitive
loudspeaker propped up on a Town
Hall chair!

On Stage
The Beatles in action on the Odeon stage in 1963.

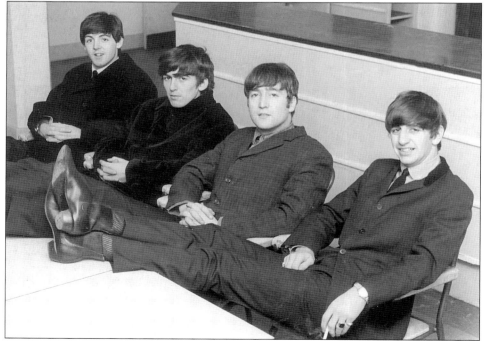

… and Backstage
As a young and rather 'green' photographer in 1963, I learned an important lesson during the Fab Four's visit to Cheltenham. My background knowledge of the Beatles was rather thin to say the least. Like everyone, I knew their music, but I was hazy about their history. Attending a photo call backstage at the Winchcombe Street cinema prior to their concert, I was disconcerted to see only four Beatles arrive on the set - turning to John Lennon, I exclaimed, 'Where's the other one? The answer he gave was curt, 'What other one, there's only bloody four of us! Duly put in my place I retreated behind the lens and resolved to swot up properly for future assignments!

Beatlemania

Some say that Beatlemania started in Cheltenham! For the three of us covering the event and stuck in the orchestra pits this was certainly an experience of epic proportions. The constant screaming from the audience was deafening! When the Beatles had given their final encore the audience rose up and raced, still screaming, to the stage. To save our own skins we leapt onto the stage and rushed for the wings. In the general confusion we were bungled into a blacked out van that sped away from the theatre with great speed across the town. It was only when we climbed out of the dark vehicle into the lights of Montpellier's Savoy Hotel that we realised we had been travelling in the company of John, Paul, Ringo and George!

Old Friends
Peter Buck Jones and Mick Bratby played in the town's premier rock group of the 1960s, The Ramrods. Here they discuss old times with a former member of the band, Brian Jones (centre), when he appeared in concert with The Rolling Stones at the Odeon in Winchcombe Street in 1964. The Ramrods' base guitarist Mick Bratby, later left the group to become a 'roadie' with The Who.

Cool Publicity Shot
Phil and The Ramrods pose for publicity photographs in a snow covered St Mary's churchyard, Charlton Kings in the winter of l963. The band, formed in 1960, consisted of (left to right), John Davies (vocals), Tony Holbrook (rhythm), Phil Crowther (lead), Peter Buck Jones (drums) and Graham 'Noddy' Stodart (bass). A year later I took photographs of Phil and his bride Christine, at their wedding. Just six days later he was dead, having choked on food while on his honeymoon. After Phil's death the Ramrods continued to play and supported many big name stars of the time, including Marty Wilde, Joe Brown, Shane Fenton, Johnny Kidd and Pirates. Forty-odd years later, this popular band are still beating out 1950s and 60s songs at venues all over the country.

Requiem for a Stone

A memorable event in pop history saw its conclusion in Cheltenham with the funeral in 1969 of Brian Jones of the Rolling Stones. The guitarist's mysterious death in a swimming pool during a party drew world-wide media attention and brought heartbreak for many fans. To this day the circumstances surrounding his death are a matter for speculation and dispute. The world's media and thousands of fans descended on the Regency Spa. In this picture Anna Wohlin (centre), Brian's girl friend, is supported by Barbara, his sister, as they make their way to the parish church. Following, just behind them, are fellow Stones, Charlie Watts and Bill Wyman (Mick Jagger and Keith Richard did not attend). It is surprising to see how many members of the older generation were also in the crowd.

Devastated fans mingled with the simply curious around the grave of Brian Jones after the burial at Cheltenham cemetery in 1969. Scenes at the graveside were mirrored elsewhere in the town as fans and media filled the town.

All types of people turned up to mourn (right).

Spitting Image (below)
Brian Jones' son Mark visiting the grave at
Bouncers Lane in 1976.

The Family of Jewellers
The Dimmer dynasty have run Martin & Co. Ltd, the town's prestigious jewellers, for over a 100 years. The firm was purchased by George Dimmer, Mayor of Cheltenham, in 1890 who went on to give a jewellery shop to each of his four sons in different parts of the country. The Dimmer's Promenade property is the safe home of the Cheltenham Steeplechase Company's valuable and historic racing trophies, their vaults housing examples dating back to the beginning of the twentieth century. Each year they commission and supply the Gold Cup for the famous March Meeting. This family picture of 1981 was taken at a jewellery exhibition organised by the family firm at the Queens Hotel. The family are (left to right), Ann and Ian, Michael and Janet, Nigel and Sally Dimmer.

Beauty and The Beast
Pete Debieux at a Cheltenham dance in the late 1970s. One of Cheltenham's colourful characters, Pete is over six feet tall has the build and image of a prizefighter and quite a reputation! I first met him in 1976 when he burst through the door of The Gloucester Old Spot Inn. Customers fell silent and averted their gaze as this giant of man, crashed across the room and, with a great bear hug, lifted the landlord off his feet! A personal grudge … an old score being settled … some sort of vendetta? One could be forgiven for thinking it was one of these, but then he broke the tense atmosphere by bursting out laughing and slapping the landlord across the shoulders, knowing full well what an effect his entrance had made on lesser mortals! In this photograph taken at a gig, with the group Left Hand Drive, at Cheltenham North Rugby Club, Pete, with dance partner Trudy, reacts in character to the intrusion of my camera. Needless to say I made a point of asking him first if he minded the picture being titled Beauty and the Beast!

End of An Era

Whittern's grocery store in Suffolk Parade, by the time it closed, was a something of a time-warp shop. Staff served customers in long white aprons and many of the shop's Victorian fittings were still in place after 141 years of trade. Fresh bowls of water were placed daily at the front door for customer's dogs and a portrait of Sir Winston Churchill still hung over the counter from 1939. Alan Whittern, whose father took over the business in 1932, is seen here on the last day of trading in the late 1980s, a closure brought on by increasing supermarket competition. When the shop's cellars were being cleared out, several cases of Commonwealth sherry came to light and I bought a few of these 'sold-as-seen' bottles. When the dust and cobwebs were wiped away, I discovered I had an Australian labelled vintage that had been produced to mark the Queens coronation. I sent the bottle to Prince Charles, with a note explaining the history of the shop and I received a letter from the palace stating that the wine, despite all those year in the cellar, was in excellent condition!

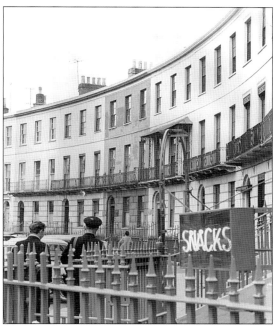

Wheels of Fortune (above)
The Royal Crescent in the 1960s. In the foreground is No. 1 which housed a basement snack bar called Tiffins. Next door was the Cheltenham Labour Club in whose basement was the Bristol Omnibus Tramway Club. In here Cheltenham-born Rolling Stone, Brian Jones, was trained to be a bus conductor. Shadows guitarist, Jet Harris, also used the club when he too worked on the Cheltenham buses. Another popular haunt was Doris's Café at the far end of the Crescent.

(top right) The original exterior of Cavendish House in the Promenade, taken in 1966, sometime before the store modernized its frontage.

Pittville Street in 1966 (right).

The Old and the New (left)
The old Pyatts Hotel in St Georges Road was virtually demolished in 1973. To preserve some of the town's regency image, the outer walls were retained, using tons of scaffolding to support the fabric, whilst a twentieth-century interior was constructed.

Phoenix Rising (bottom left)
In 1960 the Cheltenham Corporation buildings were badly damaged by fire but were restored in Regency style. This photograph taken in 1963 shows the restored façade newly unveiled after an expenditure of £317,000.

New Regency (bottom right)
The first new Regency-style houses to be built in Cheltenham since the town became famous as a spa town, were built in 1964 in Andover Road. These twentieth-century homes, designed to harmonise with the original architecture of the town, went on the market at £5,000 each.

Spa Lady
The Cheltenham Information Bureau, based in a tiny office in the Promenade was 'home' to Miss Hall, as she was known by the townsfolk. This was her original office, seen here in 1972, with just two assistants and one telephone line. She worked tirelessly to promote the town and tourism. Without fuss, she handled last minute hotel and B&B requests, dealt with inquiries for concerts and festival tickets, arranged taxi and bus trips. She was a pioneer in what is now, for Cheltenham, a multi-million pound industry. On her retirement, a galaxy of the Borough's 'Great and Good' turned out for a party in her honour, at the Pittville Pump Rooms and Miss Hall was taken there in style in a chauffeur-driven Rolls Royce.

The Italian Job
This was Cheltenham's first Italian delicatessen, opened and run by the Ferraro family; Luigi, his wife Marianna and their two sons, Costanzo and Franco seen here in 1979. The couple married in 1965, when he was working as head waiter at the Plough Hotel, a former coaching inn, situated in Cheltenham's High street and Marianna, also Italian, was housekeeper at the Carlton Hotel. In 1969 they established Luigi's Restaurant in Tewkesbury, which became a popular venue in the town and followed this ten years later with the Capri Restaurant in Cheltenham's Promenade and the delicatessen, 'Da Franco', named after their son, which they still run today in the Shurdington Road.

The Promenade
A view of the Promenade taken from the roof of the Cavendish House store in 1966. The cars give the date away as do the steps leading up to the former General Post Office on the left of the photograph.

Hitting the Roof
John and Doreen Mears established a hardware shop in Montpellier Street in the 1960s. John was instrumental in forming the Montpellier Traders Association and organised their first street fair. He applied for one of the newly created restoration property grants and to save costs decided to do the work himself, rebuilding the regency roof, while Doreen looked after the shop below. For three seasons his lone figure on the skyline was very much part of the Montpellier scene.

The Caring Duchess
The Duchess of Kent, patron of the National Star Centre College, Ullenwood, near Cheltenham, chats with students Cathryn Vallance and Harminder Singh, during one of her frequent visits to the college, here in 1981.

Loyal Support
A flag waving Winchcombe postie proudly supports the Ist Battalion of the Gloucestershire Regiment on parade in the ancient Saxon Borough during a visit to the county in the early 1960s.

On Parade
Two young would-be soldiers try to get in step with troops of the Gloucestershire Regiment as they parade through the town in the early 1960s.

A College for Ladies
Because of their green school uniform pupils of the world famous Cheltenham Ladies College, were known affectionately by townsfolk as 'Greenfly'. The college is a much more relaxed institution than in the early days of its founder, Miss Beale. The matriarch apparently imposed a silence rule on the girls.

I was allowed into the hallowed halls in 1973, when Miss Hampshire was principal of the college, to take photographs for a *Guardian* feature. This picture shows students making their way to classes through the Victorian-tiled corridors The sombre exterior of the college did not reflect the free, informal atmosphere within. I was surprised to find pin-ups of the likes of James Dean and Cliff Richard on their bedside cabinet doors!

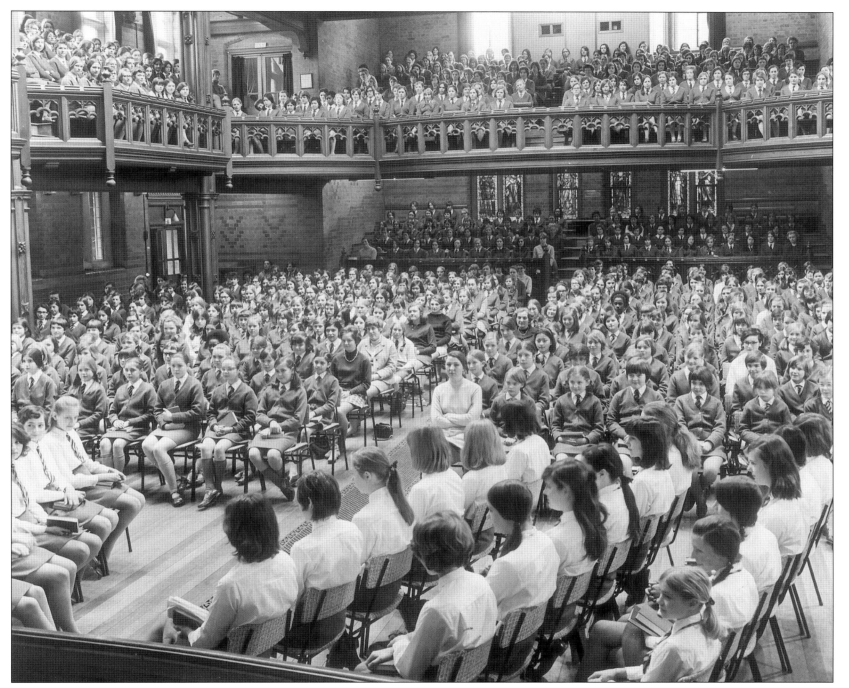

The Class of '73
Pupils of Cheltenham Ladies College prepare for the morning assembly in the Great Hall of the school.

End of Term (above and opposite)
Cheltenham Boys College mark the end of term with lunchtime drinks and family picnics on the sports field in 1982.

The Communist Lord
The Hon. Wogan Philipps, pictured in 1973 at his home Butlers Farm, Colesbourne, near Cheltenham. On the death of his father, Lord Milford, in 1962, Mr Philipps inherited the title and rocked the establishment by becoming the country's first communist peer. For his maiden speech in the House of Lords he called for its abolition and always preferred to be known by the family name. A dedicated communist, he fought against Franco in the Spanish Civil War, where he was wounded while driving an ambulance with the International Brigade. An established artist, he held several exhibitions of his work in the county.

A Child in Paradise

The centre of attention for the Merryweather family here in 1971, was newly arrived Maria, a three years old Vietnamese orphan from the Mekong Delta. The child was brought out of the war torn country by Project Vietnam Orphans and collected from Paris by mother of three, Patsy Merryweather. Maria was taken to paradise, literally, for her new found family lived in the tiny hamlet of Paradise, between Cheltenham and Stroud, complete with a pub named the Adam and Eve! Patsy holds Maria and poses with her three daughters, Jill, Celia and Alizon for an informal photo call for the local media. Maria is now thirty years of age and works for the London-based accountants, Price Waterhouse. Mr and Mrs Merryweather have now retired and live in Painswick in a house named Eden Cottage!

Massacre

Members of the Elim Pentecostal church whose British headquarters are situated in St Georges Road Cheltenham, pictured here arriving at church in 1978. They were attending a Sunday morning service on the day after twelve of their British missionaries, and a three week old baby, had been hacked to death by black nationalist guerrillas in their jungle mission school in Rhodesia.

Cheers
Ray Hughes and his wife Susan, many years his junior, dancing together on her birthday party held at Southam Tythe Barn. Ray, bought a corner shop in the Tewkesbury Road in the early 1970s and created 'The Sherry Bar', a unique establishment where customers armed with their own bottles, selected sherry from a multitude of casks around the store. The business grew considerably and had its own bonded warehouse for spirits. An astute businessman, Ray threw many parties, where the champers and wine flowed like water.

Homecoming (top)

In 1963 Colin White was cleared of a murder charge. White, in the company of two others, had given a lift to two girls hitch hiking at Combe Hill. Later one of the girls was found dead in Somerset and the three were charged with murder. The prosecuting counsel stated that 'it was unlikely that any reasonable jury would convict him' and he was acquitted. I photographed him on his return to his Charlton Kings home as he was greeted by his overjoyed mother.

(Top right) Fred Abel the travelling circus man (see p. 4).

Cotswold Ranger (right)

Walter Didcote, at sixty six, decided to clear up the highways and byways of his beloved Cotswolds. In 1972, he formed the Cotswold Rangers, a team of Robin Hood like characters complete with tartan jackets and feathered hats. They cleared away tons of rubbish and brought a successful case against a Winchcome man who, in 1973, dumped rubbush in a hedgerow. After sifting through the junk the Rangers discovered old letters bearing the culprit's name and address and he was fined £30!

Bonnie and Clyde
In July 1985, a young couple carried out an armed robbery on the General Post Office in the Promenade. Philip Ouless, twenty six, and his pregnant wife, Jayne, seventeen, almost got away with nearly £9,000 from their gun toting heist but it was not to be their day. Their exploits were brought to a halt by a rugby tackle from passing Cheltenham shopkeeper, Richard Whittaker, owner of 'That Sandwich Place' in Regent Street. He later received the Police Gold Medal for his part in bringing the couple that the media had dubbed 'Bonnie and Clyde', to book. These 'snatch' shots of the couple arriving at court were taken from a high-rise block of flats overlooking St George's Road police station. The pyjama clad tenant of the apartment I used, was not happy at being woken from his sleep at 7am but after a few pound notes had changed hands he was soon making us coffee which kept flowing until the 10 am hearing when I also 'captured' Bonnie and Clyde.

Reach for the Skies
Peter Thomas seen here in front of a Hanley Page Hastings, owned many aircraft at Staverton Airport, near Cheltenham, but they seldom left the ground! Peter was responsible for establishing the Skyfame Aircraft Museum in 1963, which he ran with his wife Gwladis. The museum owned fourteen different types of aircraft, had displays of aviation memorabilia and was set up as a tribute to his brother who died in the war. By 1977, punitive rent and rate increases had made it impossible to continue in the municipal airport hanger and so they eventually flew the Staverton nest and took the lot to Pembrokeshire.

Bike Mad
Felix and Rose Burke with one of their vintage motorcycles at their Pittville Lane in 1970. The couple took part that year in a South African motorcycle rally using a 1913 Williamson Combination which was the oldest machine in the event. A long time friend of Martyne Earle, of the Gloucester Old Spot Inn, they had both been dispatch riders in World War Two. Felix ran a scrap metal and rag business in the town and his car number plate bore the letters, 1 BOR (I Buy Old Rags).

Demolition Man
The proprietor of United Demolition, Doug Auchterloni, stands amid the rubble of the old retort housing at Tewkesbury Road gasworks, which his company demolished in 1965. A keen sportsman, Doug played rugby for Cheltenham North, was member of the Cheltenham water polo team, as well as swimming for the England water polo side from 1956 to 1966.

That's My Boy
Renowned Cheltenham pig breeder, Lionel Organ, proudly presents a future champion from a 1977 litter of his famed Southam Pedigree Large White herd. His prowess with pigs was such, that every country in the world, wanted his stock for breeding. He used to employ me to photograph his champion pigs - not an easy task. We often spent hours tempting the creatures with apples, toffee, even treacle, to get these fine but stubborn animals to pose and look their best. I usually left the farm with a gift of a dozen eggs or bag of potatoes; it was Lionel's way of apologising for his wayward youngsters!

Man of Steel (left)
Paul Egan founded FormFlo Ltd in 1970 and he was photographed here at his Lansdown Trading Estate office. He was the first managing director of the company that designed and patented a unique cold rolling metal forming process. The main advantage of this revolutionary technique over conventional methods, was the great saving in raw materials. Formflo is now a major manufacturer and supplier of components to the worldwide automotive industry.

The Landlord and the Old Spots (left and top left)
In 1978 there were three pubs in the Combe Hill area with Swan in their name so when Martyne Earle, landlord of the White Swan, bought some Gloucester Old Spots he decided to change the name of his pub from bird to porker! The popular Piff Elms pub, was decorated with all manner of old and interesting clutter, including a large copper jam-making boiler. Newcomers who asked what it was got an answer after putting two shillings in the charity box! Martyne and his wife, Mary, posed for me just before setting off for a Licencesd Victuallers ball in the late 1970s. I can disclose that he was wearing borrowed black shoes for the evening – mine!

Long Serving Lady

Joan Mitchell was born in St Pauls in 1920. As a young bride of twenty she became landlady of the Red Lion at Wainlodes Hill, the youngest licensee in the country. At that time food at the pub was prepared on open fires, lighting was by oil lamp and water was pumped from a well. Here in 1985 Joan is seen with friends and customers celebrating her 60th birthday and fortieth anniversary as mine host. She has since established a record as the county's, and one of the country's, longest serving landladies.

Smart Old Tram
This photograph recorded the finishing touches being put to Cheltenham Tram No. 21 by dedicated members of a restoration group led by John Williams (left), at their site in Leckhampton. The gleaming vehicle with its original advertising promoting Drakes Store, once situated in Winchcome Street, was donated in 1963 to the tram museum at Crich in Derbyshire.

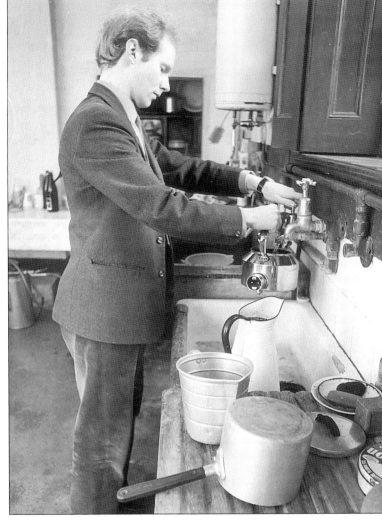

The Bed-sit Squire

In 1966, Tom Fenton, then eighteen years old, inherited Higham Court from his mother's cousin, Mark Gambier-Parry. This elegant seventeenth-century mansion and 400-acre estate near Gloucester was at first more than he could handle. For security and insurance purposes, Tom, now Lord of the Manor, initially moved into the kitchen only of the sixty-roomed pile, creating a sort of one-room, 'squire's bedsit'. Although in the near future he was to become a wealthy young man, he lived in frugal conditions for some time, until the formalities of his inheritance were sorted out. His great uncle was composer, Sir Hubert Parry, who wrote Jerusalem and also lived in the great house. In 1967 Tom became an articled pupil with G.H. Bayley and Sons, the Cheltenham firm of chartered surveyors in the Promenade. In 1971 he teamed up with the former manager of the Cheltenham Savoy Hotel, Andre Busek, to create The Restaurant Lautrec, a French-style bistro, which was a popular Montpellier venue in the 1970s. In 1978 he sold Higham Court to musician, Roger Smith, owner of T.W. Smith and Sons, the Cheltenham timber merchants.

The Faithful Wife
Mrs Rhona Prime bravely tries to carry on with a normal life, despite the presence of police at her Pittville home. Days before this picture was taken her husband, Geoffrey Prime, was arrested in Hereford on child sex charges. Returning to Cheltenham on bail, he confessed to his wife, whom he married in 1977, that for the past fourteen years he had been a Russian spy. At the time I tried to act as an intermediary between her and the media who were, not surprisingly, prepared to pay considerable fees for an interview with her. Despite my advice that, with two young boys to bring up, she should take their money, she steadfastly refused. In 1982, Prime was sent to prison for thirty-five years and the fallout from his treachery brought about the government banning of union membership at the Government Communications Headquarters (GCHQ) in Cheltenham.

On The March
The Promenade traffic was brought to a standstill as
GCHQ union protesters made their way through
town to the Montpellier Gardens in 1983. This
photograph, taken from the roof of the Queens Hotel,
shows only a small section of this huge parade that
tailed back to Pittville Street.

Solidarity (left)
The government banning of trade unions at GCHQ was fiercely contested by union members at the Oakley and Benhall spy centres. For several years, from 1983, annual rallies took place in the town with thousands of supporters descending on the borough to express there disatisfaction at the treatment of their union brothers. Here some of the sacked staff line up before making the walk from Pittville Pump Rooms to the rally marquee in Montpellier Gardens.

Cheltenham's Tolpuddle (below)
Labour Party leader, Neil Kinnock, shares a joke with TUC leader, Norman Willis, during one of the many rallies held in the town during the early 1980s, in support of the sacked trade unionists at GCHQ. Hundreds of trade unionists, annually descended on the town to protest at the union ban.

Treading the Boards (right)
Cheltenham actor Michael Shaw, pictured here in 1965, was a member of the Playhouse Company at the town's Theatre and Arts Club in Bath Road. He later played Charles Grenville, the squire of Ambridge in *The Archers*.

The Actress (far right)
Former Cheltenham Ladies pupil, Damaris Hayman in 1974 at her home in Charlton Park Gate. Damaris first appeared in Rep at Maidstone Theatre. and her many stage and television appearances since, has ensured that she has one of those instantly recognizable faces. She worked on several Childrens Film Foundation productions, including *Anoop and the Elephant,* appeared in the *Doctor Who* series and various plays for children's television. She has appeared with many of the big names in British comedy, including Charlie Drake, Tony Hancock, Les Dawson, Morecombe and Wise, Dick Emery, Dickie Henderson.

Bobby on a Bike
The Chief Constable of Gloucestershire, Peter White, on his twenty-three years old bicycle in Lansdown. This top cop was setting a good example to his fellow officers during the petrol crisis of December 1973. In 1963, Mr White started a prosecution against himself, after being involved in a road accident in Shurdington, admitting that he was to blame for the incident. He pleaded guilty, his license was endorsed and he was fined £20!

Jackboots on The Prom
The Queens Hotel was transformed into
The Hotel der Konigin, German swastika
flags fluttered above the foyer and jack-
booted soldiers marched around the streets
in 1984 when HTV filmed sequences for its
production of *Jenny's War*.

A Stitch in Time
Nigel Hawthorn, Robert Hardy,
Dyan Cannon and Elke Sommer
starred in the film. Between takes
Miss Sommer was spotted getting on
with some off stage knitting, an
activity normally considered bad luck
in the English theatre!

Respecting the Dead
The small town of Winchcombe came to a standstill on 8 February1972 for the funeral of a Gloucestershire Regiment soldier, Lance Corporal Ian Bramley, killed while on duty with the 1st Battalion in Northern Ireland. Many of the shops in the town closed their doors as a mark of respect while the sombre procession made its way to the graveside ceremony.

The Disappeared (right)
Lucy Partington, a twenty-one year old student from Gretton came home for Christmas in 1974. After visiting a friend in the Pittville area she mysteriously disappeared from the bus stop where she was last seen. Police searches and public appeals revealed no clues as to her whereabouts. At the time I was freelancing for ATV and drove Lucy's mother to the Birmingham studios for a news appeal. I recall how difficult it was to make conversation on that journey. I became further involved in the story when I was made responsible first, for locating and issuing pictures of Lucy to the press and then following police activities for television news. It was twenty years before news of Lucy's sad fate came to light. In a crowded press conference at the height of the Cromwell Street murder investigations in Gloucester, Detective Superintendent John Bennett, read out the names of four more victims discovered in the grounds at No. 25 - Lucy Partington was on the list.

Questions (far right, top)
Detectives made door to door calls Even though there was no body, the inquiry began to take on the hallmarks of a murder investigation, which many years later, it turned out to be.

The Hunt (right)
Soon after Lucy's disappearance an incident room was set up at Cheltenham Police Headquarters.

Maggie! Maggie! Maggie!
Adoring Tories greet Prime Minister Margaret Thatcher during her visit to Cheltenham in 1982 for a Party rally at the racecourse. Among my press photographer colleagues in the centre is *Echo* photographer, Richard Sturdy (left) and on the right is Johnny Moran. Johnny started as tea boy with the *Manchester Daily Express* and was considered one of the top 'snatch' men in the business. [A 'snatch' is a captured image of a person reluctant to be photographed]

One for the Scrapbook
Dedicated supporters get an opportunity to meet and take snaps of their leader.

In with the Crowd
Margaret Thatcher, being followed here by her rather anxious-looking husband, Dennis, was at the height of her powers when she made this visit in 1982. The man on the left of the picture with a camera is racecourse photographer, Bernard Parkin, who is more often to be seen snapping mounts than ministers.

Dennis and the Big Cheese
Margaret Thatcher was presented with a huge Double Gloucester cheese during her visit to Cheltenham which here appears to have been topped with the head of her husband!

Man of Trees
Henry Elwes, and his wife Carolyn, at their home, Colesbourne Park, near Cheltenham in 1972. He had demolished the decaying family home, Colesbourne Park, to make way for this modern house, designed around the panelled dining room of the old one, which was completed in 1960. This is the third house to be built on the estate. His great-grandfather, horticulturist and traveller, Henry John Elwes FRS, was responsible for introducing thousands of new trees and plants to the estate, collected on world travels. In 1972 the present Henry Elwes continued his ancestor's work by planting nearly thirty thousand more trees on the Colesbourne estate. Henry Elwes is now Lord Lieutenant of Gloucestershire.

*Castle Costume*s (right)
In 1974 an exhibition of costumes used in the popular BBC television series *The Pallisers* was opened at Sudeley Castle, Winchcombe, by actress Susan Hampshire who played Lady Glencora in the production. She is seen here looking over the displays with Elizabeth Dent-Brocklehurst, lady of the house.

Royal Connections (left)
Mark Dent-Brocklehurst, owner of Sudeley Castle with his American-born wife Elizabeth, (now Lady Ashcombe) and Adam Pollock as they toured the grounds with the Duke and Duchess of Bedford in 1970. The occasion was the launch of an exhibition at the castle titled 'Royal Sudeley'.

The Debutante and the Prince
Her Serene Highness Princess Imeretinsky in the drawing room of her Tivoli Road home in 1977. The daughter of a vicar, this former English debutante married Prince George Imeretinsky, godson of the Russian Tsar Nicholas. Prior to the Russian revolution, Prince George's parents moved to England to educate their children and the couple met at a social event when she was eighteen. After their marriage they came to live in Cheltenham. Though probably not rich they led a comfortable lifestyle in the town and the princess was active in charity work including The Distressed Gentlefolk's Association. She never visited Russia and the couple had no children so it is believed that the Georgian title died out on her death in the mid 1980s.

On the House
Les Hicks, landlord of the Royal Oak pub in Prestbury village in the1960s, hands out the traditional, warming Stirrup Cup, during a Boxing Day hunt meet at the pub. Les was a popular publican, who over the years, was Mine Host at several inns in the town.

Radio Times.

In 1977 the cast of *The Archers,* Radio Four's 'everyday story of country folk', took over the Star Inn, at Ashton-under-Hill, to record a Harvest Festival episode. The producer asked if members of the press would like to take part in the show and we all eagerly agreed. We filed into the pub's skittle alley, doubling as Ambridge church, for a hearty rendition of *We Plough the Fields and Scatter,* which was recorded and used in the broadcast!

Amazing Grace

Canon Henry Cheales had been rector at the Cotswold village of Wyck Rissington for thirty-three years when he retired to Bourton-on-the-Water in 1980. He was the son of a vicar and one of those classic English eccentrics. He created a 700-yard long maze in the rectory grounds claiming the directions came in a dream which described the pattern and gave instructions as to the location. The maze was completed in 1952 and was built round a giant Redwood tree which had been brought to England on board the SS *Great Britain* over 120 years before. The canon dealt with all things spiritual, including poltergeists! He was widely known for the exorcising of spirits and often visited the Cheltenham area to help people troubled by them. He felt they were like children, needing to be disciplined and treated in a firm manner!

Sharp Lady

There are not many lady saw doctors to be found, in fact Sue Hopton believes she is the only one in the country. In 1978, as a mother with two small boys, she started the business from the garage of her home in Haywards Road, Charlton Kings. Tradesmen were soon beating a path to her door. Within two years she bought up her nearest competitor, the Cheltenham Saw Company, and later moved her works to the Innsworth Technology Park, near Gloucester. She now employs a staff of four and although saw doctoring is still the mainstay she now offers a range of servicing for saw machinery.

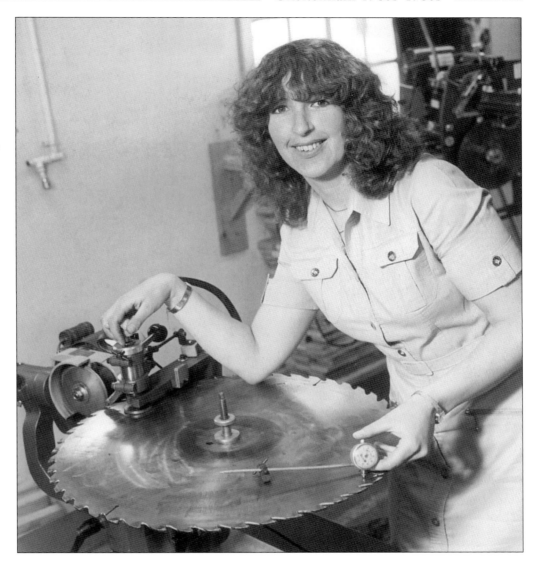

Vintage Stuff
Bill Allen hands over Winston Churchill's car.

Trombone Man
Taking every opportunity to practise on his trombone in the late 1970s was Tom Riley, landlord of The Bell Inn, Bath Road. The reason for his keenness was a forthcoming Cheltenham landlords' charity concert, the first of several in the town, when publicans were invited to do 'a turn'. Tom's rendition of *When The Saints Go Marching In* was so well received he took several encores.

Art For God's Sake
In its heyday in the 1960s, the Benedictine order of Prinknash was a thriving community. The monks ran a farm, an incense factory and a pottery works, producing a vast range of items for the abbey shop. Here in 1979, Brother Stephen applies gold leaf to one of the Prinknash designs produced to commemorate a royal event. The monk, who formerly worked with a London advertising agency, visited the abbey in 1975 for a week's 'retreat', fell in love with the way of life and joined the order.

Oh Brother
The Benedictine Order of Prinknash Abbey take their first meal in the refectory of their newly built abbey. The foundation stone was laid in 1939 and the monks moved from the old abbey, which they had occupied since 1928, in the spring of 1972. The first story I covered in Gloucestershire, was of Brother Finbar, a genial Irish monk, whose labour of love was rebuilding the crumbling Cotswold stone wall that encircled the 340 acre estate. He often paused in his task to take advantage of one of my Senior Service cigarettes!

Holy Smoke
Brother Bernard of Prinknash Abbey sifts the ingredients for making incense in 1971. From their small factory in the abbey grounds the monks sold this exotic perfumed product all over the world. In 1961, they were invited by the Sacristan of the Cave of Bethlehem to supply incense for the Christmas ceremonies and every November a small parcel of this special perfume made its way from the Cotswolds to the Holy Land. Some years later I was on the Isle of Man covering an assignment about witchcraft. As the members of the cult were dancing naked around a smoked filled magic circle, I was amazed to see a packet of the famous Prinknash incense on the table!